T0088404

The Song of Harvest

Bob Chilcott

for SATB and organ

vocal score

MUSIC DEPARTMENT

OXFORD
UNIVERSITY PRESS

OXFORD
UNIVERSITY PRESS

Great Clarendon Street, Oxford OX2 6DP,
United Kingdom

Oxford University Press is a department of the University of Oxford.
It furthers the University's objective of excellence in research, scholarship,
and education by publishing worldwide. Oxford is a registered trade mark of
Oxford University Press in the UK and in certain other countries

© Oxford University Press 2021

Bob Chilcott has asserted his right under the Copyright, Designs
and Patents Act, 1988, to be identified as the Composer of this Work

First published 2021

Impression: 1

All rights reserved. No part of this publication may be reproduced,
stored in a retrieval system, or transmitted, in any form or by any means,
without the prior permission in writing of Oxford University Press

Permission to perform this work in public (except in the course of divine worship)
should normally be obtained from a local performing right licensing organization,
unless the owner or the occupier of the premises being used already holds a licence
from such an organization. Likewise, permission to make and exploit a recording of this work
should be obtained from a local mechanical copyright licensing organization

Enquiries concerning reproduction outside the scope of the above
should be directed to the Music Rights Department, Oxford University Press,
at music.permissions.uk@oup.com or at the address above

ISBN 978–0–19–355775–8

Music and text origination by Katie Johnston

Printed in Great Britain on acid-free paper by
Halstan & Co. Ltd, Amersham, Bucks.

Contents

Composer's note iv

Texts v

1. Hymn: Come, ye thankful people, come 1
2. This is the day 6
3. Hymn: For the beauty of the earth 12
4. Gratitude 18
5. Hymn: Pray that Jerusalem may have peace 20
6. King of Glory, King of Peace 22
7. Hymn: Through all the changing scenes of life 26
8. Consider 31
9. Hymn: Now thank we all our God 35

Composer's note

Harvest season is a special time of the year. Living as I do in quite a rural part of England, each year we become ever more aware of the passing of the seasons, of the weather patterns, and also of the changing colours and textures of the land around us. After the challenges that we have all faced in 2020 and 2021, I wanted to write a simple expression to reflect on some thoughts of how the concept of harvest might relate to us all as we move forward, through sustainability, community, giving, hope, care, and, perhaps most importantly, thankfulness.

I was not specifically looking to write a stand-alone work, but rather a piece that could be equally performed as one or simply delved into and movements or hymns sung separately. It was written for the Royal School of Church Music Celebration Day, held at Durham Cathedral on 9 October 2021, as part of a day to celebrate what it means to sing together. I am grateful to Hugh Morris, Director of the RSCM, to Daniel Cook, Master of the Choristers and Organist of Durham Cathedral, and to my dear friend who supported the creation of this work.

Duration: *c.*26 minutes

This note may be reproduced as required for programme notes.

Texts

These texts and melodies may be reproduced as required for programme notes and to allow audience/congregation participation in the hymns during a performance of *The Song of Harvest*.

1. Hymn: Come, ye thankful people, come

Music: Bob Chilcott; Words: Henry Alford (1810–71)

MORRIS

© Oxford University Press 2021

1. Come, ye thankful people, come,
   Raise the song of harvest-home!
   All be safely gathered in,
   Ere the winter storms begin;
   God, our Maker, doth provide
   For our wants to be supplied;
   Come to God's own temple, come;
   Raise the song of harvest-home!

2. We ourselves are God's own field,
   Fruit unto his praise to yield;
   Wheat and tares together sown,
   Unto joy or sorrow grown;
   First the blade and then the ear,
   Then the full corn shall appear;
   Grant, O harvest Lord, that we
   Wholesome grain and pure may be.

3. For the Lord our God shall come,
   And shall take his harvest home;
   From his field shall purge away
   All that doth offend, that day;
   Give his angels charge at last
   In the fire the tares to cast,
   But the fruitful ears to store
   In his garner evermore.

4. Then, thou Church triumphant, come,
   Raise the song of harvest-home;
   All be safely gathered in,
   Free from sorrow, free from sin,
   There for ever purified
   In God's garner to abide;
   Come, ten thousand angels, come,
   Raise the glorious harvest-home!

2. This is the day

Psalm 118: 24, 28–9

This is the day which the Lord hath made: we will rejoice and be glad in it.
Thou art my God, and I will thank thee: thou art my God, and I will praise thee.
O give thanks unto the Lord, for he is gracious: and his mercy endureth for ever.

3. Hymn: For the beauty of the earth

Music: Bob Chilcott; Words: F. S. Pierpoint (1835–1917)

EXON

© Oxford University Press 2021

1. For the beauty of the earth,
   For the beauty of the skies,
   For the love which from our birth
   Over and around us lies:
   Christ our God, to thee we raise
   This our sacrifice of praise. [repeat]

2. For the beauty of each hour
   Of the day and of the night,
   Hill and vale, and tree and flow'r,
   Sun and moon and stars of light:
   Christ our God, to thee we raise
   This our sacrifice of praise. [repeat]

3. For the joy of human love,
   Brother, sister, parent, child,
   Friends on earth, and friends above,
   For all gentle thoughts and mild:
   Christ our God, to thee we raise
   This our sacrifice of praise. [repeat]

4. For each perfect gift of thine
   To our race so freely giv'n,
   Graces human and divine,
   Flow'rs of earth and buds of heav'n:
   Christ our God, to thee we raise
   This our sacrifice of praise. [repeat]

4. Gratitude

Henry van Dyke (1852–1933)

Whatever gifts and mercies in my lot may fall,
I would not measure
As worth a certain price in praise, or great or small;
But take and use them all with simple pleasure.

For when we gladly eat our daily bread, we bless
The Hand that feeds us;
And when we tread the road of Life in cheerfulness,
Our very heart-beats praise the Love that leads us.

5. Hymn: Pray that Jerusalem may have peace

Music: Bob Chilcott; Words: Scottish Psalter (1650)

PATE

© Oxford University Press 2021

1. Pray that Jerusalem may have
   Peace and felicity:
   Let them that love thee and thy peace
   Have still prosperity.

2. Therefore I wish that peace may still
   Within thy walls remain,
   And ever may thy palaces
   Prosperity retain.

3. Now, for my friends' and brethren's sake,
   Peace be in thee, I'll say;
   And for the house of God our Lord
   I'll seek thy good alway.

6. King of Glory, King of Peace

George Herbert (1593–1633), from The Temple *(1633)*

King of Glory, King of Peace,
I will love thee:
And that love may never cease,
I will move thee.
Thou hast granted my request,
Thou hast heard me:
Thou didst note my working breast,
Thou hast spared me.

Wherefore with my utmost art
I will sing thee,
And the cream of all my heart
I will bring thee.
Though my sins against me cried,
Thou didst clear me;
And alone, when they replied,
Thou didst hear me.

Sev'n whole days, not one in sev'n,
I will praise thee.
In my heart, though not in heav'n,
I can raise thee.

7. Hymn: Through all the changing scenes of life

Music: Bob Chilcott; Words: Nahum Tate (1652–1715) and Nicholas Brady (1659–1726), New Version of the Psalms of David *(1696)*

MANNERS

© Oxford University Press 2021

1. Through all the changing scenes of life,
   In trouble and in joy,
   The praises of my God shall still
   My heart and tongue employ.

2. O magnify the Lord with me,
   With me exalt his name;
   When in distress to him I called,
   He to my rescue came.

3. The hosts of God encamped around
   The dwellings of the just;
   Deliv'rance he affords to all
   Who on his succour trust.

4. O make but trial of his love,
   Experience will decide
   How blest they are, and only they,
   Who in his truth confide.

5. Fear him, ye saints, and you will then
   Have nothing else to fear;
   Make you his service your delight,
   Your wants shall be his care.

6. To Father, Son, and Holy Ghost,
   The God whom we adore,
   Be glory, as it was, is now,
   And shall be evermore. Amen.

8. Consider

Christina Rossetti (1830–94)

Consider
The lilies of the field whose bloom is brief:
We are as they;
Like them we fade away,
As doth a leaf.

Consider
The sparrows of the air of small account:
Our God doth view
Whether they fall or mount,
He guards us too.

Consider
The lilies that do neither spin nor toil,
Yet are most fair:
What profits all this care
And all this coil?

Consider
The birds that have no barn nor harvest-weeks;
God gives them food:
Much more our Father seeks
To do us good.

9. Hymn: Now thank we all our God

Music: Bob Chilcott; Words: Martin Rinkart (1586–1649), trans. Catherine Winkworth (1827–78)

PICKER

© Oxford University Press 2021

1. Now thank we all our God,
   With heart and hands and voices,
   Who wondrous things hath done,
   In whom this world rejoices;
   Who from our mother's arms
   Hath blessed us on our way
   With countless gifts of love,
   And still is ours today.

2. O may this bounteous God
   Through all our life be near us,
   With ever joyful hearts
   And blessed peace to cheer us;
   And keep us in his grace,
   And guide us when perplexed,
   And free us from all ills
   In this world and the next.

3. All praise and thanks to God
   The Father now be given,
   The Son, and him who reigns
   With them in highest heaven,
   The One eternal God,
   Whom earth and heav'n adore;
   For thus it was, is now,
   And shall be evermore. Amen.

Commissioned for the Royal School of Church Music
with the generous support of an anonymous donor and dedicated to all those
who work so hard to sustain church music now and into the future

The Song of Harvest

1. Hymn: Come, ye thankful people, come

Henry Alford (1810–71) **BOB CHILCOTT**

'MORRIS'

© Oxford University Press 2021

Printed in Great Britain

OXFORD UNIVERSITY PRESS, MUSIC DEPARTMENT, GREAT CLARENDON STREET, OXFORD OX2 6DP
The Moral Rights of the Composer have been asserted. Photocopying this copyright material is ILLEGAL.

22
win - ter storms be - gin; God, our Mak - er, doth pro - vide
29
For our wants to be sup - plied; Come to God's own
35
tem - ple, come; Raise the song of har - vest - home!
41
S.
A.
mf
2. We our - selves are God's own field,
3. For the Lord our God shall come,
T.
B.
mf
mf

48
(ORG.)
Fruit un - to his praise to yield; Wheat and tares to - ge - ther
And shall take his har - vest home; From his field shall purge a -
55
(ORG.)
cresc.
sown, Un - to joy or sor - row grown; First the blade and
- way All that doth of - fend, that day; Give his an - gels
cresc.
62
(ORG.)
f
then the ear, Then the full corn shall ap - pear; Grant, O
charge at last In the fire the tares to cast, But the
f
69
har - vest Lord, that we Whole - some grain and pure may be.
fruit - ful ears to store In his gar - ner ev - er - more.

DESCANT SOPRANOS
76
f
4. Then, thou Church tri -
ALL OTHER VOICES
f
4. Then, thou Church tri - umph - ant,
82
-umph - ant, come, Raise the song of har - vest - home;
come, Raise the song of har - vest - home; All be
88
All be safe - ly ga - thered in, Free from sor - row,
safe - ly ga - thered in, Free from sor - row, free from

94
ff
free from sin, There for ev - er pu - ri - fied
ff
sin, There for ev - er pu - ri - fied In God's
ff
100
In God's gar - ner to a - bide; Come, ten thou - sand
gar - ner to a - bide; Come, ten thou - sand
105
rit.
an - gels, come, Raise the glo - rious har - vest - home!
an - gels, come, Raise the glo - rious har - vest - home!
rit.

2. *This is the day*

Psalm 118: 24, 28–9

BOB CHILCOTT

© Oxford University Press 2021. Photocopying this copyright material is ILLEGAL.

15
mf
it.
Thou art my God, and I will
mf
mf
19
thank thee: thou art my God, and I will praise
24
f
thee, praise thee, praise thee.
f

29
T./B.
unis. f
This is the day which the
f
32
Lord hath made: we will re - joice and be glad in it.
36
f
S.
A.
This is the day which the Lord hath made: we will re - joice and be
T./B.

40
glad in it, glad in it, glad in it.
44
mp poco espress.
O give thanks un - to the Lord, for he is gra - cious,
mp poco espress.
mp
49
mf
O give thanks, for he is gra - cious: and his
mf
mf

53
mer - cy en - dur - eth, his mer - cy en - dur - eth for
57
f
ev - - er.
f
f
61 unis. f
This is the day which the Lord hath made: we will re - joice and be
unis.
f

65
glad in it. This is the day which the Lord hath
68
made: we will re - joice and be glad in it,
71
glad in it, glad in it.
ff
ff
ff
fff

3. Hymn: For the beauty of the earth

F. S. Pierpoint (1835–1917)

BOB CHILCOTT

'EXON'

© Oxford University Press 2021. Photocopying this copyright material is ILLEGAL.

16
praise, Christ our God, to thee we raise, This our sa - cri - fice of praise.
21
S./A.
unis. mf
2. For the beau - ty of each
T./B.
unis. mf
2. For the beau - ty of each hour Of the
26
hour Of the day and of the night, Hill and vale, and tree and
day and of the night, Hill and vale, and tree and flow'r, Sun and

30
f
flow'r, Sun and moon and stars of light:
Christ our God, to thee we raise This our
moon and stars of light:
f
f
34
sa - cri - fice of praise, Christ our God, to thee we raise This our
38
mf
p
sa - cri - fice of praise.
3. For the
mf
p
mf dim.
p

43
(ORG.)
joy of hu - man love, Bro - ther, sis - ter, pa - rent,
46
(ORG.)
child, Friends on earth, and friends a - bove, For all
49
mp
gen - tle thoughts and mild: Christ our God, to thee we raise This our
mp
mp

53
sa - cri - fice of praise, Christ our God, to thee we raise This our
57
sa - cri - fice of praise.
61
DESCANT SOPRANOS
f
4. For each per - fect gift of thine To our race so
ALL OTHER VOICES f
4. For each per - fect gift of thine To our race so free - ly
f

65
free - ly giv'n, Grac - es hu - man and di - vine, Flow'rs of earth and
giv'n, Grac - es hu - man and di - vine, Flow'rs of earth and buds of
69
buds of heav'n: Christ our God, to thee, to
heav'n: Christ our God, to thee we raise This our sa - cri - fice of
73
rit.
thee we raise, we raise This our sa - cri - fice of praise.
praise, Christ our God, to thee we raise This our sa - cri - fice of praise.
rit.

4. *Gratitude*

Henry van Dyke (1852–1933)

BOB CHILCOTT

© Oxford University Press 2021. Photocopying this copyright material is ILLEGAL.

15
eat our dai - ly bread, we bless The Hand that feeds
19
mf
us, that feeds us; And when we tread the road of Life in cheer - ful -
mf
23
f
-ness, Our ve - ry heart - beats praise the Love that leads us, And when we
f
27
mf
tread the road of Life in cheer - ful - ness, Our ve - ry
mf
rit.
slower
30
p
heart - beats praise the Love that leads us, the Love that leads us.
p

5. Hymn: Pray that Jerusalem may have peace

Scottish Psalter (1650)

BOB CHILCOTT

'PATE'

© Oxford University Press 2021. Photocopying this copyright material is ILLEGAL.

17
(ORG.)
And ev - er may thy pa - lac - es Pros - pe - ri - ty re -
21
DESCANT SOPRANOS
f
3. Now, for my friends' and breth - ren's
- tain.
ALL OTHER VOICES
f
3. Now, for my friends' and breth - ren's sake,
f
25
sake, Peace be in thee, I'll say; And for the house of
Peace be in thee, I'll say; And for the house of
28
rit.
God our Lord I'll seek thy good al - way.
God our Lord I'll seek thy good al - way.
rit.

6. *King of Glory, King of Peace*

George Herbert (1593–1633)
from *The Temple* (1633)

BOB CHILCOTT

© Oxford University Press 2021. Photocopying this copyright material is ILLEGAL.

24
I will love thee: And that love may ne - ver cease, I will move thee.
30
S.
Where - fore with my ut - most art I will sing
A.
Where - fore with my ut - most art I will sing thee,
34
thee, And the cream of all my heart I will bring thee.
And the cream of all my heart I will bring thee.

39 unis. mp
S./A.
Though my sins a - gainst me cried, Thou didst clear me; And a - lone, when
mp
44
they re - plied, Thou didst hear me, thou didst hear me.
mf
49
mf
Sev'n whole days, not
mf
54
one in sev'n, I will praise thee. In my heart, though not in heav'n,

59
S.
I can raise thee. King of Glo - ry, King of
A.
I can raise thee. King of Glo - ry, of Glo - ry,
f
64
Peace, King of Glo - ry, King of Peace,
King of Peace, King of Glo - ry, King of Peace,
mf
69
King of Glo - ry, King of Peace.
King of Glo - ry, King of Peace.
mp
p
rit.

7. *Hymn: Through all the changing scenes of life*

Nahum Tate (1652–1715) and Nicholas Brady (1659–1726)
New Version of the Psalms of David (1696)

BOB CHILCOTT

© Oxford University Press 2021. Photocopying this copyright material is ILLEGAL.

23
S.
A.
(ORG.)
T.
B.
mag - ni - fy the Lord with me, With me ex - alt his name;
30
(ORG.)
When in dis - tress to him I called, He to my res - cue
37
came.
unis.
3. The hosts of God en - camped a -
44
T./B.
- round The dwell - ings of the just; De - li - v'rance he af -

51
-fords to all Who on his suc - cour trust.
58
unis. mp
S./A.
4. O make but tri - al of his love, Ex - pe - rience will de -
mp
65
-cide How blest they are, and on - ly they, Who in his

72
S./A.
truth con - fide.
mf
5. Fear him, ye
T.
B.
mf
mf
78
(ORG.)
saints, and you will then Have no - thing else to fear; Make
85
(ORG.)
you his ser - vice your de - light, Your wants shall be his

91
DESCANT SOPRANOS
f
6. To Fa - ther, Son, and Ho - ly
care.
ALL OTHER VOICES
f
6. To Fa - ther, Son, and Ho - ly
f
98
Ghost, The God, the God whom we a - dore, Be glo - ry, as it
Ghost, The God whom we a - dore, Be glo - ry, as it
105
rit.
slower
was, is now, And shall be ev - er - more. A - men.
was, is now, And shall be ev - er - more. A - men.
rit.
slower

in loving memory, Shauni McGregor

8. Consider

Christina Rossetti (1830–94)

BOB CHILCOTT

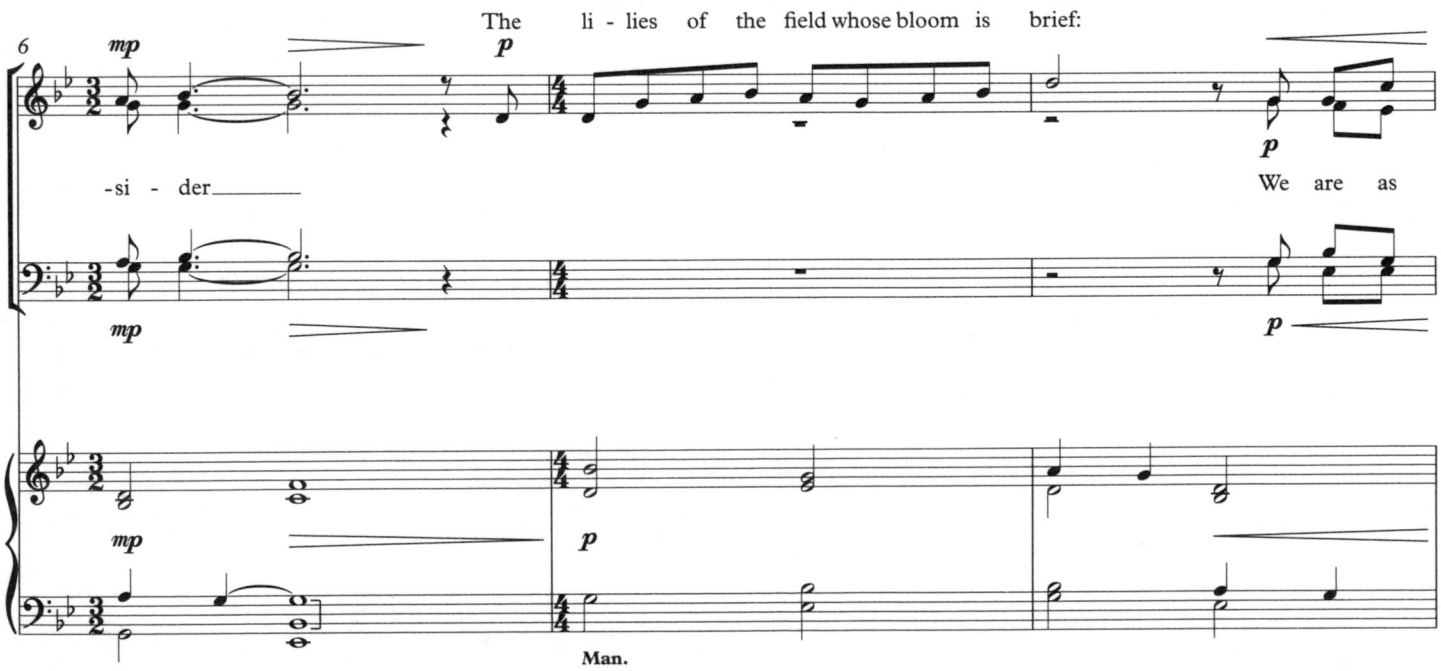

© Oxford University Press 2021. Photocopying this copyright material is ILLEGAL.

9
mp
p
they; Like them we fade a - way, As doth a leaf. Con - si - der, con -
mp
mp
p
Ped.
Man.
13
mp
p
- si - der
Our God doth
unis. p
The spar-rows of the air of small ac - count:
mp
p
Ped.
16
mp
view Whe - ther they fall or mount, He guards us too. Con - si - der the
mp
mp

20
mf
toil, Yet are most fair; What pro - fits
li - lies that do nei - ther spin nor toil, Yet are most fair; What pro - fits
mf
mf
poco rit.
a tempo
all this care And all this coil?
23
p
all this care And all this coil?
p
care, this coil?
poco rit.
a tempo
p
Man.
Ped.
27
p
mp
p dolce
Con - si - der, con - si - der The
p
mp
p dolce
mp

31
mp
birds that have no barn nor har - vest - weeks; God gives them food: Much more our
mp
34
good,
mf
Fa - ther seeks To do us good, Much more our Fa - ther seeks To do us good, to do us
mf
good, us
mp
mf
rit.
to do
38
p
pp
good, to do, to do us good.
p
pp
rit.
p
pp
Man.
Ped.

9. *Hymn: Now thank we all our God*

Martin Rinkart (1586–1649)
trans. Catherine Winkworth (1827–78)

BOB CHILCOTT

'PICKER'

© Oxford University Press 2021. Photocopying this copyright material is ILLEGAL.

16
S./A.
T./B.
mf
love, And still is ours to - day. 2. O
mf
mf
21
(ORG.)
may this boun - teous God Through all our life be near us, With
25
(ORG.)
ev - er joy - ful hearts And bless - ed peace to cheer us; And
29
(ORG.)
And
keep us in his grace, And guide us when per - plexed, And

33
(ORG.)
free us from all ills In this world and the
37
DESCANT SOPRANOS
f
3. All praise and thanks to God The
next.
ALL OTHER VOICES f
3. All praise and thanks to God The
f
41
Fa - ther now be gi - ven, The Son, and him who reigns With
Fa - ther now be gi - ven, The Son, and him who reigns With

45
them in high - est hea - ven, The One e - ter - nal God,
them in high - est hea - ven, The One e - ter - nal God, Whom
49
Whom earth and heav'n a - dore; For thus it was, is
earth and heav'n a - dore; For thus it was, is now, And
rit.
slower
ff
53
now, And shall be ev - er - more. A - men.
shall be ev - er - more. A - men.
rit.
slower
ff